Bobby the Brain

Fun Learning and Activity Book for Kids

MICHAEL AIMS

Bobby the Brain:
Fun Learning and Activity Book for Kids

Michael Aims

PUBLISHED BY RAD LEARNING BOOKS

www.RadLearningBooks.com

ISBN: 978-1-7355126-0-0

Note to Parents

Bobby the Brain has been created to help young kids learn about their amazing brains, begin to understand how it works, and develop an appreciation for their bodies and minds. While children can look through the book on their own, they will get the most out of it if you read Bobby with them and discuss what you are reading. The suggested activities at the end of the book will also help with that.

Hello!

My name is Bobby, and I am your brain—an organ that is in your head, underneath that hard shell called the skull.

Did you know

that you can listen and read this book because of the work that I do?

It's true! In fact, your brain helps your body and mind do many important jobs.

But before we talk about those jobs, you need to know a little bit more about me.

I have three major parts:

- **The cerebrum**
- **The cerebellum**
- **The brain stem**

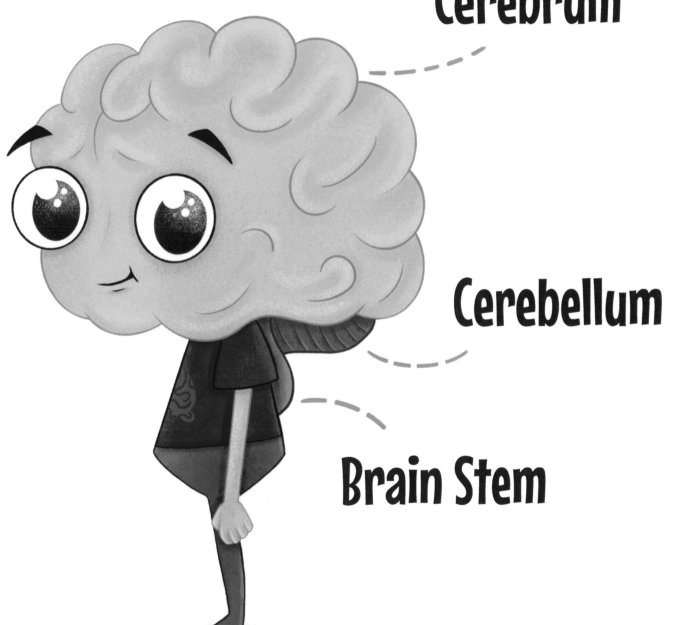

Cerebrum

Cerebellum

Brain Stem

The biggest part of me is the

cerebrum,

which controls your thoughts.

When someone asks you a question and you think of the answer, you're using the cerebrum. You also use it when you imagine something.

The cerebrum also controls your five senses:

smell, touch, taste, sight, and hearing.

So, the next time Mommy makes you eat your veggies, and they taste horrible, that is because of me!

But the cerebrum is also the reason

you can taste yummy chocolate, hear a fire siren when you watch an exciting show on television—or feel the warm fur on a dog or cat.

Another part of your brain is called the **cerebellum...** known as the "little brain." This is the part that helps with coordination.

Try this:

Throw a ball back and forth with a friend or family member five times. Did you do it?

Great job!

You just used the cerebellum to help coordinate your hands and arms to throw and catch the ball!

The cerebellum also allows you to learn new things. So, when you learned how to jump on one foot, it is because of the "little brain!"

Next is the brain stem,

which controls things that you don't think about, like breathing, digesting food, and making your heart beat. The brain stem does these things automatically for you.

Complete the following activities with your child. Have him/her read the statements in bold at the bottom of each page to reinforce the vocabulary for the different parts of the brain.

Activity Pages

Activity 1

Ask your child to walk in a straight line (make a line on the sidewalk with a piece of chalk or have him/her follow a sidewalk crack).

Look at how you kept yourself balanced! That's your little brain—the cerebellum —at work!

Activity 2

Ask your child to feel his/her heartbeat by putting his/her right hand on the left side of the chest.

Do you feel your heartbeat? Your brain stem makes your heart beat, so you don't need to think about it!

Activity 3

Ask your child to do the following:

Imagine a huge jar of your favorite cookies! Tell me what you see: What does the jar look like? What color is it? What kind of cookies are inside? What do they look like?

You were able to imagine those yummy cookies because of your cerebrum.

About the Author

During the COVID-19 pandemic, fourteen-year-old Michael Aims asked himself, "How can I help others during this time?" And the idea for Bobby the Brain was born—a book that could both entertain and educate young kids about their incredible brains!

Excelling in biology, anatomy, and English, it is not surprising that Michael has been recognized by his high school as student with exceptional capabilities. He has also won the "most innovative product award" at regional business fair for children.